D1164303
SILVER-HORN
TRIDENT
Art
Yu Mor
Original Story
Tsutomu Satc
Character design
Kana Ishida
3
THE HONOR STUDENT AT
Magic High School

# CONTENTS

The Honor Student at Magic High School

BA (BAM)
WAIT, WHAT!?
IT'S DARK ALL OF A SUDDEN!
EEEK!! I'M SCARED!
IS THIS SHADOW SQUARE!?
I CAN'T SEE ANY-THING! WHERE ARE WE!?
LET'S USE THIS CHANCE TO ESCAPE!
DA DA DA DA (TMP)
THESE SOLICITATIONS... THEY'RE SO EXTREME WE CAN'T FOLLOW TATSUYA-SAN...
YEAH... THANKS AS ALWAYS, HONOKA.
YOU'RE WEL-COME...
DA DA DA

CHAPTER 12

部活連本部
SIGN: CLUB COMMITTEE HQ
THAT CONCLUDES YESTERDAY'S INCIDENT.
BA (FWSH)
I'M VERY SORRY!
DON'T LET THE DISCIPLINARY COMMITTEE MEMBER'S CONSIDERATION GO TO WASTE—NOTHING MAJOR HAPPENED BECAUSE OF HIM.
YES, SIR!

KIRIHARA, WHY WOULD YOU DO THIS?

......
YOU MAY BE ROUGH AROUND THE EDGES, BUT YOU UNDER-STAND THE RESPONSI-BILITY THAT COMES WITH POWER.
YOU WOULDN'T USE HIGHLY DEADLY MAGIC FOR NO REASON.

......
DON'T WANT TO SAY?

I JUST DIDN'T LIKE IT.

DIDN'T LIKE WHAT?
I DIDN'T LIKE MIBU— HER SWORDS-MANSHIP.
THAT'S ALL.

IS THAT REALLY ALL?

!

...IT'D BEEN A WHILE SINCE I'D SEEN HER...
...AND HER SWORDPLAY HAD GOTTEN SO ROUGH... IT REALLY TICKED ME OFF FOR SOME REASON.

I DON'T MEAN SHE WAS BEING CARELESS...
IT WAS MORE LIKE HER SWORD HAD BECOME STRANGELY BARBARIC— *AS IF IT WAS TO KILL PEOPLE...*

IS SOMETHING WRONG WITH THAT?
WE ABANDONED THE "WAY" OF THE SWORD AND CHOSE THE "ART" OF THE SWORD.
BUT MIBU ISN'T A KENJUTSU SWORDSMAN—SHE'S A KENDO SWORDSMAN.
OUR SWORDSMANSHIP IS THE ONE FOR KILLING—NOT HERS.
HER SWORD MUSTN'T BE USED AS A MEANS TO KILL PEOPLE. IT SHOULD BE KENDO, THE WAY OF THE SWORD, THROUGH AND THROUGH.
SO YOU FEEL... THAT MIBU'S TECHNIQUE HAS GONE IN THE WRONG DIRECTION?
YES.
THERE MUST BE SOMEONE IN THE KENDO CLUB WHO CORRUPTED HER TECHNIQUE...
THAT'S WHY I COULDN'T STAY QUIET.

SO YOU PROVOKED THE KENDO CLUB.
IT ISN'T LIKE I WAS TRYING TO MAKE HER REALIZE HER MISTAKES...
...OR CORRECT THEM.
I SIMPLY LET IT GET TO MY HEAD AND PICKED A FIGHT WITH HER. I FULLY UNDERSTAND I WAS BEING IMPATIENT.
I TRULY APOLOGIZE.

I UNDER-STAND. YOU MAY LEAVE.
EXCUSE ME!

......

MIYUKI-SAN, IS THAT THE REPORT FROM THE CLUB COMMITTEE?
OH!

YES, PRESIDENT. IT JUST ARRIVED ONLINE.
OH, SO THEY DOCUMENTED KIRIHARA-KUN'S TESTIMONY, THEN.

WHY THE LONG FACE? DID THE SPEECH RECOGNITION MAKE A FEW MISTAKES?
HA HA!

NO, THAT ISN'T IT, BUT...

OH MY.
IS SOMETHING ABOUT IT BOTHERING YOU?
BOTHERING ME... PRESIDENT, HAVE YOU ALREADY READ THIS?

YES, THEY LET ME READ IT— THE REASONING IS A BIT HARD FOR ME TO UNDERSTAND THOUGH.

I SEE.
I COULDN'T UNDERSTAND IT COMPLETELY EITHER...
... BUT ...

BUT WHAT?
IF KIRIHARA-SENPAI IS RIGHT ABOUT THERE BEING A SOURCE FOR THIS "CORRUPTION"...
...I JUST THOUGHT IT WOULD BE PRETTY SCARY...

OH, YES, THAT WOULD BE SCARY.
BECAUSE OF OUR CAREER PATHS, MANY OF THE CLUBS HERE EMPHASIZE REAL-LIFE COMBAT...
...AND STUDENTS JOIN THOSE CLUBS WITH THAT UNDER-STANDING.

BUT IF KIRIHARA-KUN'S HUNCH IS CORRECT...
THEN STUDENTS COULD HAVE BEEN INSTILLED WITH PRACTICAL COMBAT TECHNIQUES WITHOUT KNOWING IT...
WHATEVER THE OBJECTIVE, IT COULDN'T HAVE BEEN FOR ANYTHING DECENT.

YOU'RE RIGHT... ONCE THE DISCIPLINARY COMMITTEE HAS SOME SPARE TIME AFTER RECRUITMENT WEEK ENDS...
...MAYBE I SHOULD HAVE MARI LOOK INTO IT A BIT.
ALL RIGHT.

I'M GOING TO STOP BY THE CLUB COMMITTEE AND ASK JUUMONJI-KUN ABOUT IT DIRECTLY.
MIYUKI-SAN, WOULD YOU CONTINUE ARRANGING THE RECORDS?
YES, I WILL.
......

I JUST HOPE THIS DOESN'T CAUSE TROUBLE FOR ONII-SAMA...

WOW, YOU CAN SEE THE WHOLE SCHOOL FROM HERE!

WE DON'T NEED TO WATCH FROM CLOSE UP! SOMETIMES YOU NEED A BIRD'S-EYE VIEW TO FIGURE THINGS OUT.

AND WITH THESE CLUB UNIFORMS ON, THE RECRUITERS WON'T PESTER US.
YEAH, YOU'RE RIGHT.

OKAY, WHERE COULD OUR LITTLE TARGET BE, THEN?
FOUND HIM. THE TREE-LINED ROAD AT THE PRACTICUM BUILDING.
OH, THERE HE IS!

MAN... IT REALLY FEELS LIKE WE'RE STALKERS, HUH?
がんっ
GAN (SHOCK)

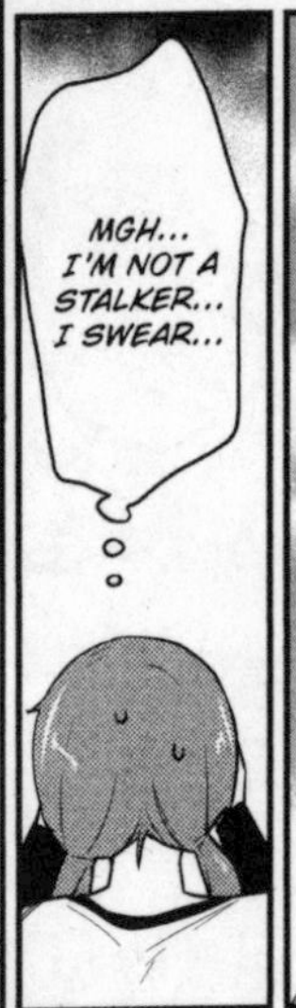
MGH... I'M NOT A STALKER... I SWEAR...

AH!

ARMBAND: DISCIPLINARY COMMITTEE OFFICER
SIGNS OF PSIONIC WAVES!
HUH?
THEY DISAPPEARED!?

WAS THAT CAST JAMMING JUST NOW...?
IT WAS, WASN'T IT?
YEAH, THE SAME AS AT YOUR HOUSE, SHIZUKU...
THE ONE YOUR BODY-GUARD WITH THE ANTINITE RING USED...

BUT OUR MAN DOESN'T APPEAR TO HAVE ANY ANTINITE.
YOU'RE RIGHT...
...

ACK, HE RAN AWAY!
IT'S THE ATTACKER! THE TREES TO THE RIGHT, IN THE SHADE!
!!
BA (WHP)
ばっ
NO, I WON'T MAKE IT!
SHIN (SILENCE)
シン…

DID YOU SEE HIS FACE?
I SAW IT! PERFECTLY!
DOON (TA-DAA)
どーーん
I THINK IT WAS THE CAPTAIN OF THE BOYS' KENDO CLUB.

WAIT, REALLY!?
I'LL HAVE TO CHECK A PICTURE OR SOME-THING, BUT I'M PRETTY SURE IT WAS HIM.
A PICTURE...
THEY MIGHT HAVE ONE AT THE STUDENT COUNCIL.
S.S.F
S.S.F

YOU WANT TO SEE PROFILES OF THE CLUB PRESIDENTS?

YEAH...

I COULD GET THEM IF I CHECKED THE STUDENT COUNCIL DATABASE... BUT WHY?
UMM, I JUST WANT TO KNOW WHAT KIND OF PEOPLE THEY ARE...

BUT HAVEN'T YOU AND SHIZUKU ALREADY DECIDED ON A CLUB TO JOIN?
W-WELL, WE DID, BUT...

...OH, I SEE. YOU WANT TO DOUBLE UP, DON'T YOU? YOU TOO, SHIZUKU?
UMM, DOUBLE UP...?
I HEARD THAT, EVERY YEAR, ABOUT 10 PERCENT OF NEW STUDENTS ENROLL IN MORE THAN ONE CLUB...AM I WRONG?
KYOTON (BLINK)
きょとん
WE'RE JUST THINKING ABOUT IT—WE HAVEN'T DECIDED YET.
TH-THAT'S RIGHT! BUT I'D BE CONCERNED IF THE CLUB PRESIDENT WAS SOME-ONE LIKE YOROZUYA-SENPAI...

A DANGEROUS REMARK, HONOKA.
KUSU (GIGGLE)
くすくす
KUSU
Auu...
KAAAA (BLUSH)
かあああ
BUT PERSONALITY INFORMATION ON INDIVIDUALS IS PRIVATE, SO I CAN'T SHOW THEM TO YOU.

YEAH...I THOUGHT NOT.
GAKU (SLUMP)
がく…
I'M SORRY, HONOKA.
OH, BUT...
...IF YOU JUST WANT THEIR PHOTOGRAPHS AND ATHLETIC RECORDS, THEY SHOULD BE ON THE PR COMMITTEE'S SCHOOL WEBSITE...
PR COM-MITTEE?
SCHOOL WEB-SITE?
?

I GUESS NOBODY TOLD YOU...
PA (BAM)
ぱっ
!

...THIS WAS A THING...

IT'S LOCKED DURING CLASSES, SO MAYBE THAT'S WHY YOU DIDN'T NOTICE IT.
I'LL GO BACK TO THE HOME SCREEN AND TRY IT AGAIN, SO LOOK CAREFULLY.
OKAY, THANKS!

......
THAT'S ODD...
I HAVE A BAD FEELING ABOUT THIS...

YEAH, THAT'S THE ONE WHO RAN AWAY!
NO DOUBT ABOUT IT!

KINOE TSUKASA FROM 3-F...
WHAT WAS HIS MOTIVE? JEALOUSY?
THAT WOULD BE STRANGE.

HE'S IN CLASS F.
OH, RIGHT!

MAYBE HE'S MAD SOMEONE FROM THE SAME COURSE 2 GOT AHEAD OF HIM?
BUT THE FIRST GROUP WE SAW WAS MADE UP OF COURSE 1 STUDENTS.

I HESITATE TO SAY THIS, BUT...I DON'T THINK THAT COURSE 1 AND COURSE 2 STUDENTS WOULD JOIN FORCES.
COULD THEY SET ASIDE THEIR EVERYDAY CONFLICT JUST TO BULLY AN UNDER-CLASSMAN?

IT'S MORE LIKE UNCONSCIOUS DISCRIMINA-TION THAN CONFLICT.
...THOUGH, I GUESS MORISAKI-KUN AND THE OTHERS MADE IT INTO AN ACTUAL CONFLICT.
FROM AN OUTSIDER'S PERSPECTIVE, WE WERE PART OF THAT...

WE'RE GETTING OFF TOPIC...
SIGGHHH—
はあ——
WELL, IF THEY CAN'T WORK TOGETHER, THEN DOES THAT MEAN MORE THAN ONE GROUP IS AFTER HIM?

More than one...
ZUUUN (GLOOOM)
ず——ん
UH...

CAN THE THREE OF US KEEP UP WITH MORE THAN ONE GROUP...?
NO, DEFI-NITELY NOT.
STILL ...

...TATSUYA-SAN MAY BE STRONG, BUT IF A BUNCH OF PEOPLE PULL A SURPRISE ATTACK ON HIM...
...HE MIGHT GET HURT AT SOME POINT.

AND THINKING ABOUT HOW SAD MIYUKI WOULD BE IF THAT HAPPENED...

I'VE GOTTA THINK OF SOME-THING I CAN DO.
SOME-THING...

OH!

WHAT IF WE TOOK A PICTURE OF THE ATTACKER AT THE SCENE OF THE CRIME!?
BA (BAM)
ぱっ
A PICTURE!?

THEN WE'D TURN INTO STALKERS FOR REAL...
N-NO! WE'RE JUST TRYING TO GET EVIDENCE!

GOOOO (ROOOOAR)
ゴオオオ
BUT WE'D BE TAKING THE PICTURE TO THE STUDENT COUNCIL, WOULDN'T WE?
DIDN'T WE JUST SAY HOW BAD THAT COULD GO?
WASN'T THERE AN ANONYMOUS REPORTING SYSTEM...?
LIKE A SCHOOL VERSION OF THE PUBLIC REPORTING SYSTEM?
YEAH, LIKE THAT!
NOT YOU TOO, SHIZUKU...

PON (PAT)
ぽん
GIVE IT UP.
YOU CAN'T STOP HONOKA WHEN SHE'S LIKE THAT.
BIKU (TWITCH)
FIRE—

URGH...

HAH...
HAH...
WHY DOES IT HAVE TO BE LIKE THIS ...!?
YEAH!

SIGN: SHIBA

COULD YOU TELL ME A LITTLE ABOUT YOUR CLASSMATES MITSUI-SAN AND KITAYAMA-SAN?
!?

THE
HONOR
STUDENT
AT
Magic High
School

STUPID! FATTY!
WHAT DID YOU SAY!?

MIYUKI, ARE YOU CLOSE...
...WITH YOUR CLASSMATES MITSUI-SAN AND KITAYAMA-SAN?
!?

YES, OUT OF ALL MY CLASSMATES, THOSE TWO ARE THE ONES I AM CLOSEST TO...
BUT WHAT ABOUT THEM?
ONII-SAMA'S CURIOUS ABOUT OTHER WOMEN?

THEY'RE NORMAL GIRLS, RIGHT?
I MEAN, THEY DON'T HAVE WEIRD INCLINATIONS AND ACT SENSIBLY, RIGHT?
!?
IN THAT SENSE... THEN THEY'RE NORMAL, I BELIEVE.
WHAT DOES HE...?

CHAPTER 13

HAVE THOSE TWO BEEN CAUSING YOU SOME SORT OF TROUBLE, ONII-SAMA?
NO, NOT AT ALL.
GOGOGOGO (RUMBLE)
CALM DOWN.
SARA (STROKE)
...

SARA
さら
SARA
さら
SO
(SLIDE)
す
I THINK THEY'VE BEEN WATCHING ME WHILE I'M ON PATROL.
I WAS JUST WONDERING WHAT THEY WERE UP TO.
YOU SAW THEM?
YES— THOSE TWO AND ONE OTHER...
A FEMALE STUDENT WITH VIVID RED HAIR WAS WITH THEM.
TING

ARMBAND: DISCIPLINARY COMMITTEE OFFICER

IT FELT LIKE THEY WERE TRYING TO GET A PICTURE OF THE PERSON MESSING WITH ME.
IS THAT TRUE?
THERE ARE MORE WHO WOULD HARM YOU, ONII-SAMA!?
SAAA (HISS)

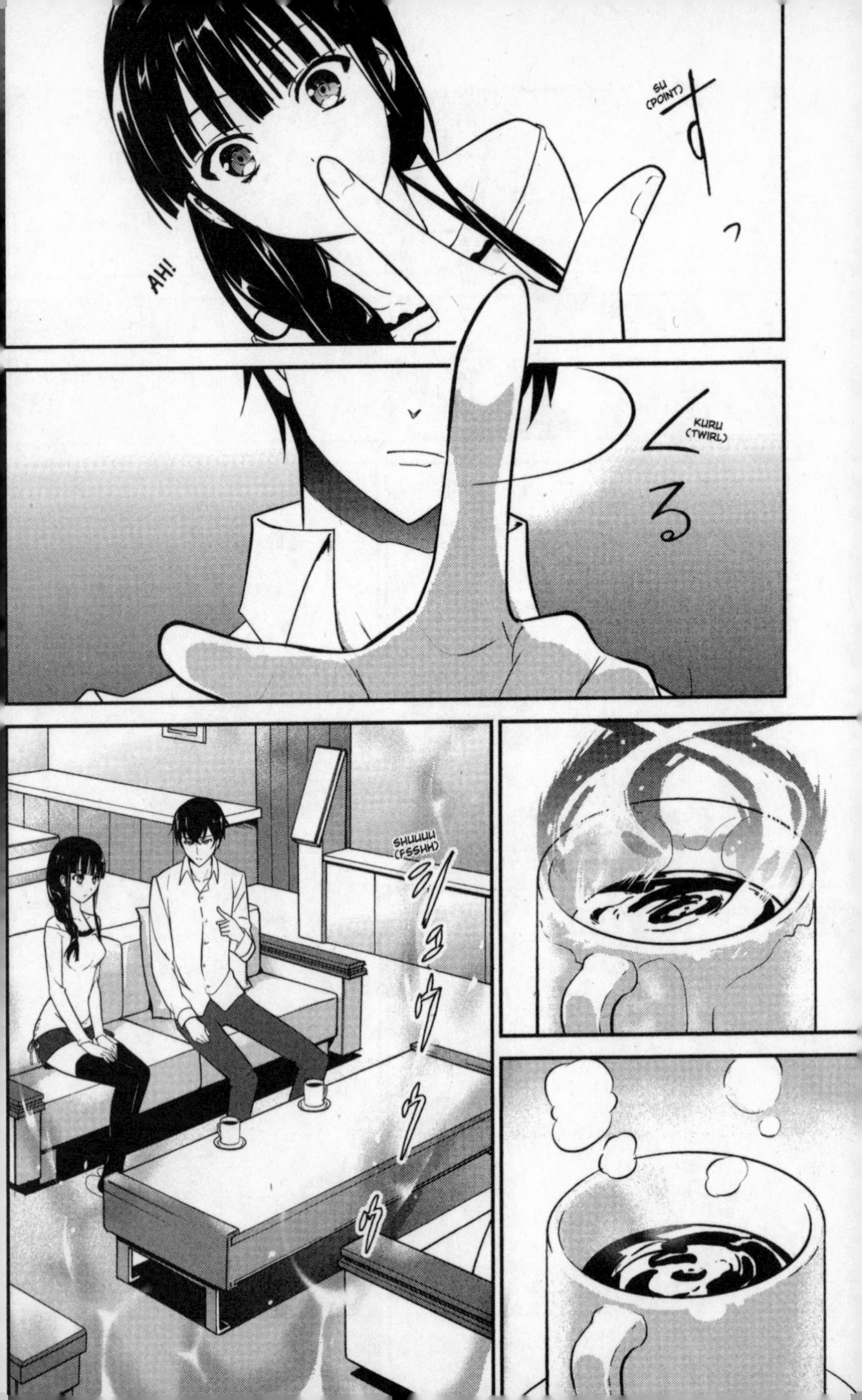
SU (POINT)
AH!
KURU (TWIRL)
SHUUUU (FSSHH)

...I AM VERY SORRY.
DON'T WORRY ABOUT IT.
I HAVEN'T BEEN INJURED AT ALL...
...BUT I WAS JUST WONDERING WHAT THEY WERE THINKING.
IF THESE WERE JUST HIGH SCHOOL PRANKS, THEN THAT'S FINE...
...BUT IF NOT, AND THEY STICK THEIR NECKS IN TOO FAR...
ONII-SAMA?
MAYBE I'M OVERTHINKING THIS.

I WONDER WHY...
...I'M FEELING UNEASY, LIKE I DID YESTERDAY...

SIGN: STUDENT COUNCIL ROOM
生徒会

MARI, COULD YOU TAKE A LOOK AT THIS?
IT CAME TO THE PUBLIC NOTIFICATION WINDOW YESTERDAY.

WHAT, SEXUAL HARASSMENT DURING RECRUITMENT?

?
CHAIRWOMAN?
IT LOOKS LIKE THIS HAS SOMETHING TO DO WITH YOU, TATSUYA-KUN.

!
"TATSUYA SHIBA-SAN, A DISCIPLINARY COMMITTEE MEMBER, WAS CAUGHT IN AN ACCIDENTAL MAGIC ATTACK.
"THIS IS THE PROOF OF THAT.
"PLEASE ENACT STRICT PUNISHMENT."
THIS, HUH...?
SO IT WAS THIS...

HM? WHAT'S THE MATTER?
NOTHING— I JUST DON'T THINK WE CAN DO ANYTHING ABOUT IT.
WE CAN'T?
THE ONLY THING DEPICTED HERE IS THE PERSON RUNNING AWAY.
IT ISN'T ACTUALLY PROOF.
THAT'S TRUE.
WE CAN'T TELL IF THIS PERSON WAS AFTER TATSUYA-KUN FROM THIS PHOTOGRAPH.
AND WE CAN'T EVEN DETERMINE WHETHER MAGIC WAS ACTUALLY USED, CAN WE?

STILL...
...YOU SURE ARE A POPULAR ONE, TATSUYA-KUN.

SURREPTITIOUS PHOTOGRAPHY IS ONE THING, BUT I DON'T PARTICULARLY WANT VIOLENT FANS.
NIYA (SMIRK)
NIYA

HONOKA AND THE OTHERS WERE THINKING ABOUT IT THIS MUCH...
I'M HAPPY THEY'RE WORRIED ABOUT ONII-SAMA, BUT...
...MAYBE I SHOULD OFFER A PIECE OF ADVICE...
...THEN AGAIN...

GAYA (CHATTER)
DID THE STUDENT COUNCIL SEE THE PICTURE WE SENT?
I WONDER WHAT HAPPENED...
GAYA
GAYA

YOU CAN'T JUST ASK. IT WOULDN'T BE ANONYMOUS ANYMORE.
SHIZUKU WARNED ME ABOUT THAT ALREADY.

MIYUKI!
WOW, CALLING HER THAT STILL MAKES ME NERVOUS!

MAYBE I COULD CASUALLY STRIKE UP A CONVER-SATION AND SEE HOW IT GOES.

OFF TO THE STUDENT COUNCIL AGAIN?
RECRUITMENT WEEK IS OVER, BUT YOU DON'T GET A REST, HUH?
I CAN'T HELP IT—IT'S AN IMPORTANT JOB.
ARE YOU AND SHIZUKU GOING TO YOUR CLUB NOW?
YEP.

I'M NERVOUS, SINCE I DON'T REALLY HAVE MUCH FAITH IN MY PHYSICAL ABILITIES...

DO YOUR BEST!
BUT BE CAREFUL NOT TO HURT YOURSELF.

I knew it! She's an angel!
OKAY! I'LL DO MY BEST!

LET'S GO, HONOKA!
SEE YOU TOMORROW, MIYUKI!

OH, SHIZUKU!
WHAT?
...NO, NEVER MIND. I'LL SEE YOU TOMORROW.
OKAY, BYE!

I HOPE THEY DON'T GET INTO SOMETHING DANGEROUS...

MIYUKI WAS ABOUT TO SAY SOMETHING.
HUH!? WAS SHE!?
IT WENT RIGHT OVER MY HEAD...
YES, BUT SHE STOPPED.

I MEAN, THINGS SEEMED NORMAL.
MAYBE IT WASN'T WORTH THEIR ATTENTION?
THEY MIGHT JUST HAVE A LOT OF REPORTS TO MANAGE AND HAVEN'T GOTTEN TO IT YET.
KA (CLACK)
KA
KA

1-E
KA
KA
EXCUSE ME, BUT DO YOU HAVE A SECOND?
YES, WHAT IS IT?
TATSUYA SHIBA-KUN IS IN THIS CLASS, RIGHT?
SORRY, BUT COULD I GET YOU TO CALL HIM FOR ME?

HE'S NOT IN THE CLASSROOM.
I THINK HE'S WITH HIS LITTLE SISTER.
HIS SISTER? MIYUKI SHIBA-SAN FROM CLASS A?
YEAH.
THANK YOU!
PEKO (BOW)

KA
KA

HMM!
KUSU (GIGGLE)

IT FEELS COMPLETELY DIFFERENT WHEN YOU GET UP TO CLASS D.
LIKE I'M BEING MADE FUN OF BECAUSE I'M A COURSE 2 ...!
KA (CLACK)
KA
CHAPTER 14

ZAWA (MURMUR)
THAT'S SHIBA FROM THE DISCIPLINARY COMMITTEE.
ZAWA
OH, YOU MEAN THE ONE...
...WHO BEAT THE KENJUTSU CLUB ACE?
NO WAY. A COURSE 2 COULD NEVER BEAT A COURSE 1 ...
TA (TAP) TA TA
I'M VERY SORRY, ONII-SAMA!
YOU ENDED UP HAVING TO WAIT FOR ME...
PON (PAT)
DON'T WORRY ABOUT IT... WELL, YOU PROBABLY CAN'T DO THAT, CAN YOU...?

SHIBA-
KUN!
TA (TAP)
だ TA
た TA
た
KURU (SPIN)
くる
HELLO!
OR I GUESS I SHOULD SAY, "PLEASED TO MEET YOU"?

SU (SSK)
YOU'RE RIGHT— NICE TO MEET YOU.
MIBU-SENPAI, IS IT?

YES, I'M SAYAKA MIBU, FROM CLASS E, *LIKE YOU*, SHIBA-KUN.

THANKS FOR BEFORE.
PIKU (FLINCH)

SORRY FOR NOT THANKING YOU WHEN YOU HELPED ME BACK THERE.

THERE'S SOMETHING I WANT TO TALK TO YOU ABOUT TOO...
COULD YOU SPARE A BIT OF TIME TO COME WITH ME?

I CAN'T RIGHT NOW.

HUH?

きょとん
KYOTON (STARTLED)
I CAN IN FIFTEEN MINUTES THOUGH.
UMM...OKAY, THEN I'LL BE WAITING IN THE CAFETERIA.
ALL RIGHT.
......
MIYUKI, SHALL WE GO?

SIGN: STUDENT COUNCIL ROOM
生徒会室
OKAY, I'LL BE WAITING IN THE LIBRARY.
THE LIBRARY?

THAT WAS THE PLAN— WHY DO YOU ASK?
WELL, YOU WERE GOING TO MEET WITH MIBU-SENPAI IN THE CAFETERIA AFTER THIS, SO...

IT CAN'T BE ANY-THING TOO TIME-CONSUM-ING.
SHE PROBABLY WANTS TO RECRUIT ME OR SOME-THING ALONG THOSE LINES.
...IS THAT REALLY ALL IT IS?
WHAT ELSE COULD IT BE?

I HAVE A FEELING IT'S NOT JUST A SIMPLE RECRUITMENT OFFER FROM HER CLUB.
I DON'T HAVE A REASON.
IT'S JUST... I FEEL RATHER ANXIOUS.

I'M VERY HAPPY THAT YOU'VE WON A REPUTATION...
...BUT IF PEOPLE KNEW EVEN A FRACTION OF YOUR REAL POWER...
...THERE WOULD BE MANY FLOCKING TO USE YOU FOR THEIR OWN ENDS.

THOSE WHO WOULDN'T WOULD BE IN THE MINORITY.
ONII-SAMA, PLEASE TAKE EXTRA CARE.
GYU (GRIP)

DON'T WORRY.
I'LL BE FINE NO MATTER WHAT HAPPENS.
THAT'S WHY I'M SO WORRIED!

I READ THE REPORT FROM THE CLUB COMMITTEE.
SO...

...IT'S OKAY.
I'D NEVER ABANDON MYSELF TO DESPAIR AND GO CRAZY.

THAT'S A PROMISE, ONII-SAMA.
ALL RIGHT.

...BY THE WAY, MIYUKI, I DON'T THINK SOME COMMITTEE ACTIVITIES IN HIGH SCHOOL ARE ENOUGH TO WARRANT ME "WINNING A REPUTATION."
!
KURU (TWIRL)
...GEEZ! WHAT DOES IT MATTER, REALLY!?

TO ME...
かあぁ
KAAA (BLUSH)
...YOUR VERY NAME IS FAMOUS, ONII-SAMA!

THE NEXT DAY, AFTER-NOON
SO?
ニヤ NIYA (SMIRK)
ニヤ NIYA
WHAT'S ALL THIS I'VE BEEN HEARING ABOUT YOU VERBALLY ABUSING SAYAKA MIBU IN THE CAFETERIA?
HMM, TATSUYA SHIBA-KUN?

Verbal abuse!?

UNFOUNDED ACCUSATIONS!
AND PLEASE STOP TEACHING SUCH VULGAR WORDS TO MY SISTER.
Onii-sama, you do know how old I am, right?
OH, IS THAT SO?

THERE WERE PEOPLE WHO SAW MIBU...
...WITH HER FACE BRIGHT RED, ALL EMBARRASSED.

THAT MEANS IT'S—
ZAA (ZZZAH)

ONII-SAMA...

ALL THIS COLD WITHOUT EVEN A C.A.D...!?
SHE DID THIS BEFORE TOO...
BIKU (JOLT)
PISHI (FREEZE)
GOGOGO (RUMBLE)

...JUST WHAT IS SHE...?
YOUR MAGICAL INFLUENCE IS QUITE STRONG, ISN'T IT...?
I'M SORRY! I WAS JUST KIDDING!

SO (PAT)
CALM DOWN, MIYUKI. I CAN EXPLAIN, ALL RIGHT?

I TRULY APOLOGIZE...
SHUUU (FSSHH)
THERE I GO AGAIN...

THEY DO SAY STRONG MAGIC COMES CLOSE TO BEING SUPER-NATURAL, BUT...
I GUESS YOU DON'T NEED AN AIR CONDITIONER IN THE SUMMER!

ALLOW ME TO EXPLAIN...
...EXACTLY WHAT HAPPENED.

AS YOU KNOW, SAYAKA MIBU IS THE KENDO CLUB MEMBER WHO GOT INTO A FIGHT WITH KIRIHARA YESTERDAY DURING THE STRUGGLE BETWEEN THE KENDO AND THE KENJUTSU CLUBS.
SHE SAID SHE INVITED ME BECAUSE SHE WANTED TO THANK ME AND ALSO BECAUSE SHE HAD SOMETHING TO DISCUSS.
PEKO (BOW)
ALLOW ME TO THANK YOU AGAIN FOR LAST WEEK.
BECAUSE OF YOU, THINGS STOPPED BEFORE GETTING OUT OF HAND.
YOU DON'T NEED TO THANK ME. IT'S MY JOB.
NO, I DON'T MEAN FOR JUST STOPPING KIRIHARA-KUN.

NEITHER SIDE WAS PUNISHED DESPITE OUR ACTIONS— THAT WAS BECAUSE YOU RESOLVED IT PEACEFULLY, RIGHT?
AND IT'S NOT NORMAL TO TAKE DOWN THAT MANY PEOPLE WITHOUT HURTING THEM.
I LET KIRIHARA-KUN GET HURT.
BUT... IF YOU DO MARTIAL ARTS ENOUGH, THIS KIND OF THING HAPPENS.
KIRIHARA-KUN SHOULD HAVE UNDERSTOOD THAT.
AND YET, SOME PEOPLE MAKE A BIG DEAL OUT OF IT.
THERE ARE A LOT OF PEOPLE WHO HAVE GOTTEN IN TROUBLE OVER SIMILAR MATTERS...
...JUST SO THE DISCIPLINARY COMMITTEE MEMBERS COULD GET BETTER GRADES!

I WONDER IF IT'S JUST ME...

...BUT THE PRESIDENT SEEMS LIKE SHE KNOWS SOMETHING...

I CAN'T STAND THE WAY THEY DESPISE MY SWORD SKILLS JUST BECAUSE I'M NOT GOOD AT MAGIC.
I WON'T LET THEM DENY WHO I AM!
THAT'S WHY...
...THE NON-MAGIC CLUBS DECIDED TO COORDINATE.
THIS YEAR, WE'RE GOING TO ANNOUNCE TO THE SCHOOL THAT MAGIC ISN'T EVERYTHING.

I WANT YOU TO HELP US TOO, SHIBA-KUN!
I SEE...
WHAT'S GOING ON?
IT'S THAT DISCIPLINARY COMMITTEE FRESHMAN...
I HAVE A QUESTION FOR YOU, IF YOU DON'T MIND.
AFTER TELLING THE SCHOOL WHAT YOU THINK...
...WHAT WILL YOU DO THEN?
!

I COULDN'T GET AN ANSWER FROM HER.
......

SHE SEEMS A BIT RADICAL, CONSIDERING ALL THAT GRADES STUFF.
HMM.
I SEE.
IS SOMEONE LEADING HER TO THINK THAT WAY...?
WATANABE-SENPAI IS STRUGGLING WITH HER WORDS TOO...?
THE STUDENT COUNCIL DEFINITELY KNOWS SOMETHING.
I WONDER IF NAKAJOU-SENPAI KNOWS TOO.
...

BY "SOMEONE"...
AH.

...ARE YOU REFERRING TO AN ORGANIZATION SUCH AS BLANCHE?

HUH?
WHY DO YOU...!?
WHAT'S BLANCHE?

UH.
UM.
GUESS SHE DOESN'T.

I SUPPOSE THERE'S NO POINT IN HIDING IT.
OUR SCHOOL IS BEING UNDERMINED BY ÉGALITÉ, A LOWER BRANCH OF BLANCHE, AN ANTI-MAGIC INTERNATIONAL POLITICAL GROUP.

!
......

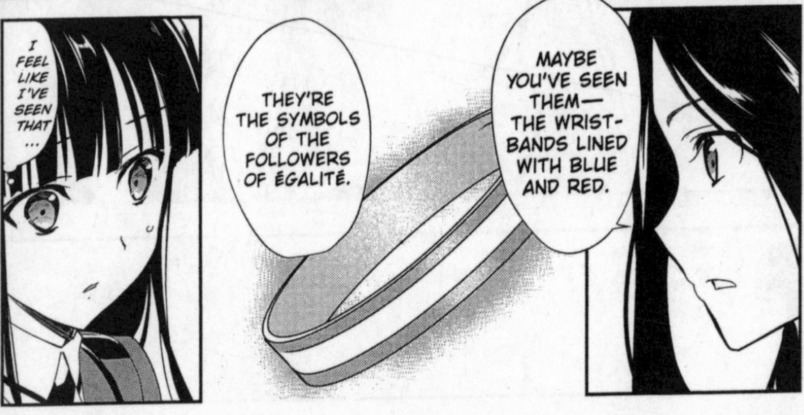
MAYBE YOU'VE SEEN THEM—THE WRIST-BANDS LINED WITH BLUE AND RED.
THEY'RE THE SYMBOLS OF THE FOLLOWERS OF ÉGALITÉ.
I FEEL LIKE I'VE SEEN THAT ...

OH!

IT WAS IN THE PICTURE HONOKA AND THE OTHERS TOOK...!
ONII-SAMA WOULD CERTAINLY HAVE REALIZED THE TRUTH BEHIND HIS ATTACKER.
IS THAT WHY HE SUGGESTED BLANCHE?

BUT WHEN WE TALKED ABOUT HONOKA AND THE OTHERS AT HOME...
...HE DIDN'T SAY ANYTHING ABOUT BLANCHE.
THE REASON WAS PROBABLY... TO PROTECT ME...

ONII-SAMA THINKS OF ME AS MORE IMPORTANT THAN ANYTHING ELSE...
...AND BECAUSE OF THAT, HE'S WILLING TO GET HIMSELF HURT.

SIGN: STUDENT COUNCIL ROOM
生徒会室
I MAY BE A SELFISH SISTER, LETTING MY BROTHER'S CONSIDERATION GO TO WASTE, BUT...
GYU (CLENCH)
...I...

ONII-SAMA!
DO YOU HAVE SOME TIME TONIGHT?
KI (GLINT)
...DON'T WANT ONII-SAMA TO GET HURT!

THE
HONOR
STUDENT
AT
Magic High
School

KIIN (SQUEAK)
THEY HAVE THESE IN NORTHERN EUROPE, DON'T THEY?
ICE HOTELS...?
NEVER THOUGHT I'D EXPERIENCE ONE IN JAPAN...

THIS CHOCOLATE CAKE HERE, PLEASE.
CERTAINLY!
SEND IT TO THIS ADDRESS IN TWO HOURS.
PI (BIP)

I'M NOT TRYING TO BROWNNOSE HER OR ANYTHING...
...BUT MIYUKI'S BEEN UNUSUALLY WORKED UP TODAY.

# CHAPTER 15

THANK YOU FOR THE DELICIOUS CAKE, ONII-SAMA.
WELL, YOU DO ALWAYS MAKE ME DELICIOUS FOOD, MIYUKI.

THIS MUCH IS NOTHING IF IT MEANS SEEING YOU HAPPY.
かあっ
KAA (BLUSH)

ぽぽぽ
POPOPO (SIZZLE)
WAS IT THAT OBVIOUS ...?
I MUST LOOK LIKE A CHILD, GETTING EXCITED OVER SWEET THINGS...

OH!
I NEED TO ASK HIM!

ONII-SAMA, ABOUT TODAY...
RIGHT, ABOUT BLANCHE... SORRY FOR MAKING YOU ANXIOUS BY NOT MENTIONING IT.
OPEN CABINET NAMED "BLANCHE."
THE ANTI-MAGIC POLITICAL GROUP, BLANCHE...ON THE SURFACE, THEY PROCLAIM THEMSELVES A CIVIC MOVEMENT...
...BUT THEY'RE ACTUALLY FULL-BLOWN TERRORISTS.
THEIR SLOGAN IS THE ABOLITION OF SOCIETAL DISCRIMINATION.
THEY CRITICIZE THE AVERAGE PAY OF MAGICIANS FOR BEING HIGHER THAN EVERYONE ELSE'S.
THAT'S...

...SUCH A RUDE OUTLOOK.
IT'S ONLY THE HIGH-EARNING MAGICIANS BRINGING UP THE AVERAGE. DO THEY NOT UNDERSTAND HOW DIFFICULT THE WORK IS FOR THOSE PEOPLE?
AND THERE ARE PLENTY OF MAGICIANS UNABLE TO USE THEIR MAGIC FOR ANY PROFIT, WHO END UP LIVING IN POVERTY OR BEING KILLED AS RESEARCH SPECIMENS.

KOKU (NOD)
BLANCHE, HOWEVER, USES THE IDEA OF EQUALITY TO COMPLAIN THAT MAGICIANS BEING PAID FOR THEIR MAGIC IS UNFAIR.
MAGICIANS HAVE LIVES TOO.
DON'T THOSE PEOPLE KNOW MAGIC CAN'T BE USED WITH INBORN TALENT ALONE?

AND WHAT I DON'T UNDERSTAND IS HOW THERE ARE PEOPLE AFFILIATED WITH BLANCHE'S BRANCH ORGANIZATION ÉGALITÉ AT FIRST HIGH.
WHY WOULD PEOPLE STUDYING MAGIC BE WITH A GROUP THAT REJECTS IT?

DO THEY NOT REALIZE WHAT THE MAGIC OPPOSITION FACTION'S ACTUALLY AFTER?
NO, I THINK THEY DO— BUT THEY'RE LYING TO THEMSELVES.

THE MINDS OF PEOPLE ARE WEAK.
BLANCHE TAKES ADVANTAGE OF THAT WEAKNESS.

SIGNS FROM TOP TO BOTTOM: A SAFE SOCIETY / NO TO MAGIC / HUMAN WORLD... / ...NORMAL PEOPLE

SIGN: NO TO MAGIC

MAGIC IS POWER, FOR BETTER OR WORSE...
...THE SAME AS FINANCIAL POWER, TECHNOLOGICAL POWER, OR MILITARY POWER.

SO THEN THESE ANTI-MAGIC ORGANIZATIONS LIKE BLANCHE...
...WANT TO MAKE THIS COUNTRY ABANDON MAGIC AND CAUSE IT TO LOSE STRENGTH?
PROBABLY.

AND THE TEN MASTER CLANS WOULD NEVER LEAVE THEM BE...

...ESPECIALLY NOT...
...THE YOTSUBA FAMILY.
BIKU (JOLT)

IN THE WORST CASE, THE YOTSUBA COULD EMBARK ON A PURGE AND POSSIBLY GET US INVOLVED IN IT.
ACTUALLY, GETTING US "INVOLVED" DOESN'T DO IT JUSTICE.

...ALL IN FRONT OF THE OTHER MASTER FAMILIES, LIKE THE SAEGUSA AND THE JUUMONJI.

OUR AUNT COULD USE US AS PURE PAWNS OF THE YOTSUBA...
BUT THAT'S...

WE WOULD CEASE TO BE HIGH SCHOOL STUDENTS.

BURU
WE WOULD NEED TO GO BACK TO THE YOTSUBA.
BURU (TREMBLE)
SU (SSK)

SO (PAT)
THERE'S NO NEED TO FEAR.
HOWEVER MANY STAND AGAINST US, I WILL NOT LET THEM DESTROY OUR LIVES.

AND IF IT BECOMES NECESSARY...
...I WILL DEAL WITH THIS BEFORE THE YOTSUBA MAKE A MOVE.

ONII-SAMA...
...THANK YOU...
FOR NOW, THE MOST IMPORTANT THING IS NOT TO GET INVOLVED CARELESSLY.

IF PRESIDENT SAEGUSA RESOLVES IT...
...THAT WOULD BE THE MOST CONVENIENT THING FOR BOTH US AND OUR AUNT.
SO FOR THE TIME BEING, WE NEED TO BE EXTRA CAREFUL.

KIIIN (DING)
KOOON (DONG)
NO NEWS SINCE THEN, HUH...?
AFTER WE WENT THROUGH ALL THAT TO GET THE PICTURE!
UGH!
MAYBE THEY DIDN'T TRUST AN ANONYMOUS REPORT...
SIGH...
THAT TOO...

"THAT TOO"?
THERE WAS NO MAGIC IN THE PICTURE IN THE FIRST PLACE.
OH...

AND IT DIDN'T SHOW HIM TRIGGERING ANY.
OH, YEAH...

What the heck are we even doing...?
Yeah...
SHOBOOOON (GLOOOOM)
しょぼーーん

I GUESS WE COULDN'T DO IT OURSELVES.
BUT THE TRUTH IS THAT FOUL PLAY HAPPENED.
THE ATTACKER DIDN'T FEEL RIGHT AT ALL, SO I DON'T WANT TO LEAVE IT LIKE THIS.

SU (SSK)

AH!
WH- WHAT?

HISO HISO (WHISPER)
OVER THERE, SEE? IT'S THE CAPTAIN OF THE KENDO CLUB.
HUH? FROM THE PICTURE?

WAIT, WE HEARD IN CLASS THAT THE KENDO CLUB HAD PRACTICE TODAY...
KOKU (NOD)
REALLY!?

SUSPICIOUS! I THINK I GET IT!
HMM.

WANT TO FOLLOW HIM A LITTLE?
YEAH, I'M CURIOUS.
NO OBJECTIONS HERE.
ALL RIGHT...

THE GIRL
DETECTIVES
BEGIN THEIR
INVESTIGA-
TION!

THE
HONOR
STUDENT
AT
Magic High
School

WE MAY HAVE BEEN BORN ON DIFFERENT DAYS...
...BUT WHEN WE DIE, IT SHALL BE TOGETHER!
?
THAT WON'T HAPPEN ANYTIME SOON.

I WONDER WHERE HE'S GOING.
HE'LL BE OUTSIDE THE SCHOOL'S SURVEILLANCE SYSTEMS SOON.
YOU'RE RIGHT...

DO YOU THINK HIS HOUSE IS IN THIS DIRECTION?
NO...I SAW HIM COMING TO SCHOOL IN A CABINET THIS MORNING, SO I DON'T THINK SO.

I KIND OF...
...FEEL A LITTLE UNEASY.
ME TOO, ACTUALLY.
YOU TOO, AMY!?
I WON'T SAY I'M PERFECTLY CONFIDENT MYSELF...
...BUT...

CHAPTER 16

ZAWA (MURMUR)
I WONDER IF THIS SHOP WILL DO.
ZAWA
ZAWA

KUSU (GIGGLE)
AHHH, I MESSED UP THE ORDER!
THE NEXT DELIVERY IS NEXT WEEK, AND THEY DON'T SELL IT ONLINE...
I CAN GO AND BUY IT.
I'M SORRY, I'M SORRY!
PEKO (BOW)
PEKO
THAT NAKAJOU-SENPAI...
HM?
THAT'S...

...HONOKA AND THE OTHERS.
I WONDER WHAT'S GOING ON.
WHOOPS, I WAS IN THE MIDDLE OF SOME-THING.

I'M GETTING A BAD FEELING...
I HOPE THEY DON'T GET INTO ANY DANGER.

YES— I'VE LED THEM TO THE SPECIFIED POSITION.

TA (DASH)
AH!
DID HE NOTICE US!?
DUNNO! LET'S FOLLOW HIM!
WHAT?
WHERE'D HE GO...?
BUON (VROOM)

DORUN
(WROOM)
GYUN
(GRRRRR)
GYUN
DO
DO
(BRR)
WH—
WHO THE HECK ARE YOU!?

LISTEN, YOU TWO...

ON MY SIGNAL, WE RUN.
OKAY.
SWITCH ON YOUR C.A.D.s.
PI (BIP)
PI

......
SNIFFING AROUND IN SOMEONE ELSE'S BUSINESS, ARE YOU?
PI
SO YOU'RE THE RATS GETTING IN THE WAY OF OUR PROJECT...

GO!!
!
DA (DASH)
DON'T LET THEM ESCAPE!

KI (KREE)
IF YOU THINK I'M A NORMAL HIGH SCHOOLER...
GWAH!
DON (SLAM)
...THEN YOU'RE SORELY MISTAKEN!

DA (DASH)
!
AMY!
MY TURN!
PREEMPTIVE SELF-DEFENSE!
KA (FLASH)
SHIT, MY EYES...!

DAMN!
YOU MONSTERS!
TAKE THIS!
KYAAAH!
KIIIII (KREEEEEEEEEEE)
WHAT'S GOING ON...!? MY HEAD IS SPLITTING APART...

HONOKA!
...!
HAAHH...
HA-HA. HURTS, DOESN'T IT?
ZA (TMP)

WE BORROWED THESE FROM TSUKASA-SAMA.
AS LONG AS WE HAVE CAST JAMMING THANKS TO THIS ANTINITE...
...YOU CAN'T USE MAGIC AT ALL!

GUESS IT'S NOT STRONG ENOUGH FOR YOU.
UGH!
DO
DO (THUD)
KH!
SHOULD WE FINISH 'EM OFF?
YEAH, LIKE WE PLANNED.
CHA (SHING)
ALL WHO GET IN THE WAY OF OUR PLANS MUST DISAPPEAR.
THIS WORLD HAS NO NEED FOR MAGICIANS!!

GET AWAY FROM MY CLASSMATES.
SHUUUUU (SHWOOSH)
!?
BARIN (CRACK)
MY KNIFE...

GOGOGO
(RUMBLE)
ゴゴゴ
AGH!
BA
(JOLT)
ばっ
WHEN DID SHE ...?
WAS THAT HER!?

IMPOSSIBLE! THIS ANTINITE IS EVEN PURER THAN THE REGULAR STUFF! YOU SHOULDN'T BE ABLE TO USE MAGIC...
HEY! TURN IT UP!
IT WON'T WORK.
CAST JAMMING? YOU'RE NOT EVEN MAGICIANS.
IT WILL NOT WORK ON ME.

YOU'RE BLUFFING—
UWAHH...!
DO
DO (THUD)

IT'S ALL RIGHT NOW.
ぽー
POOO (DAZED)
Miyuki came to rescue us...
Is this a dream?
YOU'RE AWAKE.
ぎゅっ
GYU (SQUEEZE)
I'M GLAD EVERY-ONE'S SAFE.

THANK YOU, MIYUKI! YOU REALLY SAVED US!
ALLOW ME TO SAY THANK YOU AS WELL, MIYUKI.
SERIOUSLY, THANKS A BUNCH!
OH, AND NICE TO MEET YOU!

I ONLY KNOCKED THEM OUT—THEIR LIVES ARE IN NO DANGER.
I THINK THE SURVEILLANCE SYSTEMS WILL FIND THEM, BUT...
...SHOULD WE REPORT THIS TO THE POLICE?

...I HAVE REASONS TO NOT WANT TO MAKE TOO BIG A DEAL OUT OF THIS...

...BUT SINCE YOU WERE ALL VICTIMS, I WILL NOT STOP YOU FROM TAKING LEGAL ACTION.
NO, THAT'S FINE. IT WASN'T ON CAMERA ANYWAY.
I SEE... THANK YOU.

MIYUKI WAS AMAZING!
IT WAS LIKE THE CAST JAMMING DIDN'T WORK AT ALL!

Her interference magic is out of this world!
YOU'RE RIGHT.
SHE'S ON THE LEVEL OF THE TEN MASTER CLANS.

HUH? DID YOU SAY SOME-THING?
NO, IT'S NOTHING.

BY THE WAY, I WAS JUST WONDERING...
...WHAT WERE THOSE "REASONS" SHIBA-SAN TALKED ABOUT?

SELECT TECH-NIQUE "PSIONIC SHIELD."
SELECT TECH-NIQUE "SONIC INSULA-TION."
...THAT SHOULD DO IT.
RRRRRING!
Who is it?
HELLO, THIS IS MIYUKI SHIBA.
IS THIS YAKUMO-SENSEI?
HOW UNUSUAL FOR YOU TO CALL ME, MIYUKI-KUN.

WHAT'S UP?
I truly apologize for my rudeness in calling you so suddenly.
There is a matter I would like your assistance with.
SURE— I'LL HELP IF I CAN.

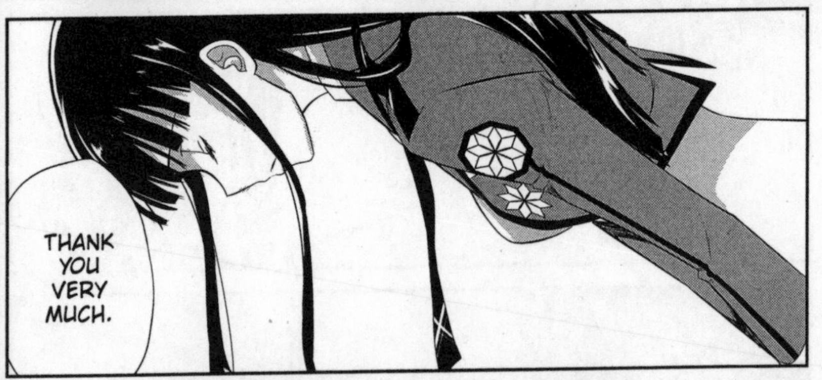
THANK YOU VERY MUCH.

A LITTLE WHILE AGO, MY CLASSMATES WERE ATTACKED BY RUFFIANS CLOSE TO THE SCHOOL.
Close to First High? How bold of them.
THEY WERE IN POSSES-SION OF ANTINITE.

I SEE...NOT JUST YOUR EVERYDAY HOODLUMS, THEN.
Still, I'd expect nothing less of you, Miyuki-kun—to be completely unfazed by cast jamming.
NO...UNLIKE ONII-SAMA, I JUST BRUTE FORCE EVERYTHING.
No, not at all. It's fantastic.

And so, where are those people now?
I LEFT THEM ON THE GROUND WITH PARALYSIS WAVE.
IN OTHER WORDS...
...YOU WANT ME TO TAKE CUSTODY OF THESE RUFFIANS BEFORE THE POLICE OR ANY OF THEIR ALLIES GET THERE?

!

YOU SEE THROUGH JUST ABOUT EVERYTHING, SENSEI.

YOU GIVE ME TOO MUCH CREDIT. NO MATTER HOW MUCH I INVESTIGATE YOU TWO, I HAVEN'T GOTTEN ANYTHING.

THE FACT YOU'RE THIS SERIOUS...
...HA-HA— IT MUST HAVE TO DO WITH TATSUYA-KUN.

Yes...

I KNOW HOW YOU FEEL, BUT LEAVE THE INTERRO-GATION TO US.

THESE SORTS OF THINGS ARE NEVER PRETTY.

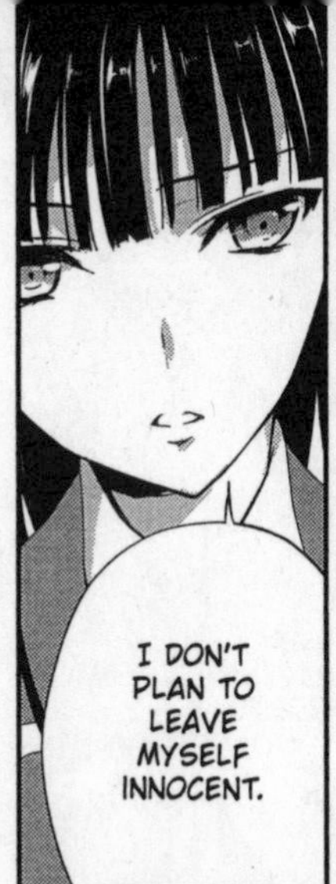
I DON'T PLAN TO LEAVE MYSELF INNOCENT.

I think Tatsuya-kun would prefer otherwise.
!

Sensei, you're mean for talking about Onii-sama!
HA HA HA!

DON'T WORRY. THE TIME WILL COME WHEN WE'LL NEED YOUR STRENGTH, MIYUKI-KUN.

Anyway, that's how it is— leave it to us this time.
ALL RIGHT.

THOSE FOUR HAVEN'T RETURNED?
NO, WE BELIEVE THEY HAVE BEEN CAUGHT...
BY THE POLICE?
WE WOULD HAVE RECEIVED WORD OF THAT.

WAS IT INTERNAL AFFAIRS? PUBLIC SAFETY...?
NO, THEY WOULDN'T CARELESSLY INTERFERE WITH THEM.

WELL, FINE. CONTINUE SEEKING THEM OUT.
UNDER-STOOD.
WE MAY NEED TO MAKE SURE THEY NEVER TALK AGAIN, AFTER ALL...

I'M SORRY FOR CAUSING YOU TROUBLE, NII-SAN...

KINOE, YOU'RE NOT THE ONE AT FAULT HERE.

SIGH.
IT REALLY IS DIFFICULT TO REFORM PEOPLE'S ELITISM THROUGH PEACEFUL TECHNIQUES LIKE TALKING.
BUT PERHAPS THE TIME HAS COME.

AH!
NII-SAN, THEN...

KINOE, ROUSE OUR COMRADES AT FIRST HIGH TO ACTION.
!

THEN WE'RE FINALLY ...!?

YES. ALL OUR PREPARATIONS ARE COMPLETE.

WHEN THE CHAOS IN THE SCHOOL REACHES ITS CLIMAX, WE WILL INSERT OUR IMPLE-MENTATION UNIT.

The Honor Student at Magic High School

I ACTUALLY SNUCK MY WAY IN! ♡
MISS PHANTOM IS SO STEALTHY!

I'M OFF TO F.L.T.
SORRY, BUT I'LL BE BACK LATE.
NO, PLEASE DON'T WORRY ABOUT IT.
OKAY...
...I SHOULD GET GOING AS WELL.

IT'S ONII-SAMA'S BIRTHDAY SOON...
I WONDER IF I SHOULD GET HIM A MATCHING HELMET.

OH!
THAT HELMET!
THE KIND THE RUFFIANS WERE WEARING YESTERDAY...!?

THAT ONE? WE HAVEN'T SOLD A SINGLE ONE OF THEM.
I SEE...
AS EXPECTED, I'LL HAVE TO ASK THEM...

THE TIME WILL COME WHEN WE'LL NEED YOUR STRENGTH, MIYUKI-KUN.
LEAVE IT TO US THIS TIME.
THAT'S WHAT SENSEI SAID...
...BUT I CAN'T JUST LEAVE IT TO THEM, AFTER ALL.
HOW ODD.
SHIN (SILENT)
MIDDAY AND NOBODY AROUND...
MIYUKI-KUN!

GUWAN (SHOUT)
I TOLD YOU TO LEAVE IT TO US, DID I NOT?
!
GO HOME FOR TODAY.
COME TO THINK OF IT, I HEARD ONCE FROM ONII-SAMA THAT THERE'S SOMETHING THAT CAN CAUSE DAMAGE WITH JUST A VOICE, USING TENGU TECHNIQUES...
WHAT A LOUD VOICE... AND IT HURTS...!
IF THIS IS MAGIC...
...THEN IF I TURN MY AREA INTERFER-ENCE ALL THE WAY UP...!

GUNYA (VWRRT)

EEEK...!
BIKU (JOLT)

WERE THEY HERE THE WHOLE TIME...!?
DON'T SCREAM LIKE THAT—YOU'LL SCARE MY STUDENTS.

S-SENSEI! I'VE ASKED YOU BEFORE NOT TO SNEAK UP ON ME LIKE THAT...
BA (FWIP)
ACTUALLY, I WAS BEHIND YOU FOR A WHILE.

YOU'RE STILL CURIOUS ABOUT IT, HUH?
WELL, I HAVE NO CHOICE, THEN—COME WITH ME.

KOTSU (CLICK)
I WOULD HAVE PREFERRED YOU TO KEEP OUT OF THIS, MIYUKI-KUN.
KOTSU
KOTSU

I'M SORRY FOR BEING SO SELFISH.
NO, IT'S OKAY.

JUST STAY FIRM, GOT IT?
NII (SMIRK)
GOKU (GULP)

THESE ARE TRAINING ROOMS WE MADE FOR MEDITATION.
THEY BLOCK ALL STIMULI FROM OUTSIDE, SUCH AS LIGHT, SOUND, AND SMELL...
...AND THEY'RE SET UP SO THAT SUBTLE VIBRATIONS EMANATE FROM THE FLOOR, WALLS, AND CEILING TO MAKE PEOPLE ANXIOUS.

WELL, IT'S NOT REALLY ALL THAT BAD, SO DON'T WORRY.
GII (KREE)

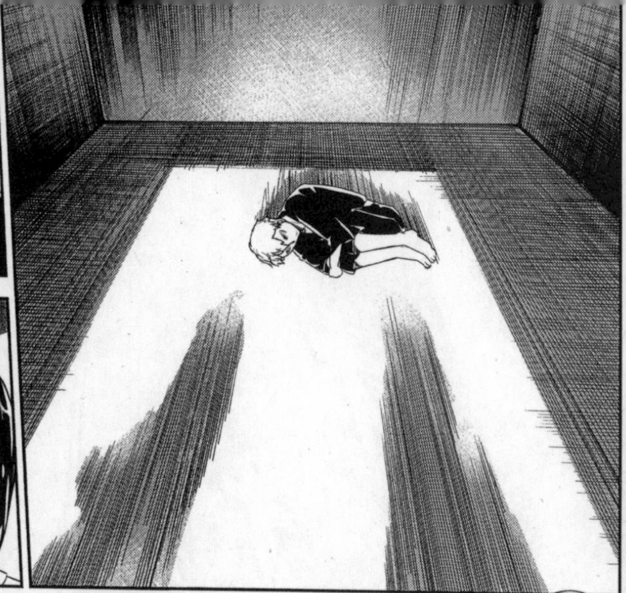

HE'S ALL RIGHT—HIS LIFE ISN'T IN DANGER.
HOW-EVER...

HOW ABOUT IT? FEEL LIKE TALKING?
HAH!
DAMN MONSTERS! YOU'RE GONNA DESTROY THE WORLD SOMEDAY!
WE WON'T LET THAT HAPPEN!
KUWA (SHOUT)
HE'S BEEN LIKE THIS... QUITE THE FANATIC, ISN'T HE?
I WANT TO RESOLVE THIS PEACEABLY, BUT...

WHAT IS YOUR NAME?
SU (SSK)

I HAVE NO NAME TO GIVE TO THE LIKES OF A MONSTER!
BIKU (JOLT)
OH MY.
OOO (LOOM)
YOU'RE ACTING RATHER RUDE TO A MONSTER, DON'T YOU THINK?

UWAAAAAHHHH!!

G...GET AWAY...
...YOU MON-STER...!
EEE-EEE-EEE-EE!!

DA (DASH)
I'LL DO ANYTHING! PLEASE HELP ME!
BA (FWIP)
BURU (TREMBLE)
BURU
LOOKS LIKE THE LUNA STRIKE WAS A LITTLE TOO EFFECTIVE.
...
KU KU
I THOUGHT MENTAL INTERFERENCE-TYPE MAGIC WAS YOUR SPECIALTY.
I MAY BE PREDISPOSED TO IT, BUT I DON'T HAVE MANY CHANCES TO PRACTICE...
THAT'S WHY I WENT TOO HARD ON HIM.
GATA (SHIVER)
GATA
WELL, IT LOOKS LIKE HE'LL TALK TO US NOW.

BUT WITH YOU HERE, MIYUKI-KUN, IT'LL HAVE THE OPPOSITE EFFECT—SO WOULD YOU MIND QUIETLY LEAVING FOR TODAY?
MY!

BIKU (JOLT)

...YOU ARE RIGHT, OF COURSE. I WILL EXCUSE MYSELF.
SA (HIDE)
SA

STILL, HOWEVER...

...HOW RUDE OF YOU TO ACT SO TERRIFIED AT THE SIGHT OF A GIRL'S FACE.

KU
KU
KU!

IF THIS CAN BE RESOLVED WITHOUT HARM COMING TO ONII-SAMA, THEN...

Attention, all students!
We are a coalition trying to abolish discrimination at school!
ZAWA (MURMUR)
WAIT, WHAT?

DO THEY NEED YOU FOR THIS?

SO IT WOULD SEEM.

But the discrimination in school goes deeper than just magic practice.

For example, the budget given to competitive magic clubs far exceeds that of the other clubs!

We learn magic because we want to be magicians ...
...but we are also high school students!
Magic isn't the only thing that matters to us!
We demand to convene with the opposition—the student council and Club Committee—and discuss the abolition of discrimination.
Until our demands are accepted, we—
ARMBAND: DISCIPLINARY COMMITTEE OFFICER
HONOKA, SHIZUKU, I NEED TO GO. I'LL SEE YOU TOMORROW.
OKAY, BYE.
I MUST HURRY...
GOOD LUCK, MIYUKI!
...BEFORE OUR AUNT APPEARS, AT ANY COST...

THE NEXT DAY
HEY, DID YOU HEAR? THE STUDENT COUNCIL PRESIDENT IS GOING TO HAVE A SHOWDOWN WITH THE GUYS FROM YESTERDAY'S BROADCAST IN FRONT OF THE WHOLE SCHOOL!
MIYUKI, ARE YOU GOING TOO?
YES... I DON'T PARTICULARLY WANT TO THOUGH.
YOU DON'T WANT TO?
I MEAN, I'M NOT INTERESTED ...
...IN PEOPLE WHO THINK THEY'RE ALLOWED TO DO ANYTHING THEY CONSIDER THEIR PRINCIPLES.
WHAT DO YOU THINK OF WHAT THE COALITION WANTS?
THEY'RE NAIVE.
IF THEY WANT TO BE HIGHLY THOUGHT OF, THEN THEY SHOULD SHOW RESULTS FIRST. IF THEY WANT RECOGNITION OUTSIDE OF MAGIC, THEN THEY SHOULD SHOW THE RESULTS OF OTHER THINGS.
SAYING THEY DESERVE MORE VALUE, BECAUSE THEY WEREN'T TREATED EQUALLY— IT'S LIKE THEY'RE TRYING TO BRING DOWN THOSE WHO ACTUALLY ACHIEVED HIGH STATUSES BY PROVING THEMSELVES. IT GIVES ME THE CREEPS.

I AGREE WITH WHAT YOU'RE SAYING, MIYUKI...
I DIDN'T REALIZE YOU WERE SO MERCILESS ON THE INSIDE.

THAT'S RIGHT.
I AM A COLDHEARTED WOMAN.
NIKO (SMILE)
OH YOU!
AGAIN WITH THE JOKES!

STILL, HMM.
THAT SURPRISED ME! MIYUKI CAN JOKE LIKE THAT TOO, HUH?
YEAH...

I THINK MIYUKI WAS A LITTLE DIFFERENT THAN USUAL.

SHE WAS KIND AS ALWAYS, BUT...
...NOW THAT YOU MENTION IT...

GOGOGO (RUMBLE)
AGH!
I WONDER IF IT HAS TO DO WITH BEFORE...
UWAH

I CAN'T STAY CALM...
I WONDER IF THERE'VE BEEN ANY DEVELOPMENTS ON YAKUMO-SENSEI'S END...

MIYUKI, I'M GOING OUT FOR A BIT.
ALL RIGHT— WHERE ARE YOU GOING?
TO SEE MASTER.
PIKU (FLINCH)
KINOE TSUKASA...THE GUY HONOKA AND THE OTHERS REPORTED TO THE STUDENT COUNCIL EARLIER...
...I'M CURIOUS ABOUT HIM.

ONII-SAMA, UMM, MAY I GO WITH YOU?
I DON'T MIND... BUT WHY?
BECAUSE I'M CURIOUS AS WELL. AND THERE'S HONOKA AND THE OTHERS TO THINK ABOUT...

ALL RIGHT. THERE'S NOT MUCH TIME UNTIL WE HAVE TO LEAVE, SO GET CHANGED QUICKLY.
YES— I WILL INFORM SENSEI THAT I'LL BE IMPOSING ON HIM AS WELL.
OKAY, THANKS.
SURU (SLIP)
FUWA (FLOAT)
EXCUSE ME FOR CALLING SO LATE.
Good evening, Miyuki-kun. What's up?
I'M SORRY, SENSEI, BUT I'D LIKE TO COME WITH MY BROTHER TO THE TEMPLE TONIGHT.

Sure, I don't mind.
THANK YOU VERY MUCH, SENSEI.

ピタ
PITA (PAUSE)
す
SU (SSK)
そ
SO (REACH)

HEY, GOOD EVENING...

OVER HERE, TATSUYA-KUN.

...TATSUYA-KUN...
PEKO (BOW)
...MIYUKI-KUN.

YOU SIBLINGS SURE ARE SOMETHING.
THE PRANA BOTH OF YOU HAVE...

MIYUKI-KUN'S PRANA GLITTERS AND SHINES, KNOWING NO BOUNDS...

...AND THERE ISN'T A SINGLE UNNECESSARY DROP OF TATSUYA-KUN'S PRANA OUTSIDE HIM.

SENSEI...
AND CONNECTING YOU—

WHOOPS, SORRY, NOT ALLOWED TO GO THERE.
NO, I APOLOGIZE AS WELL.

SO WHAT HAVE YOU COME TO ASK ME?

DO YOU KNOW ANYTHING ABOUT A SECOND-YEAR AT FIRST HIGH NAMED KINOE TSUKASA?

IT WOULD BE FASTER TO GO THROUGH COLONEL KAZAMA AND ASK THE YOUNG LADY FUJIBAYASHI...
...OUR AUNT WOULD NOT THINK WELL OF THAT.

I SEE. THAT'S QUITE A BIND, ISN'T IT?

THEN I'LL TELL YOU WHAT I KNOW.
KINOE TSUKASA'S OLD NAME WAS KINOE KAMONO.
HIS FAMILY, A BRANCH FAMILY OF THE KAMOSHI, IS DESCENDED FROM ONMYOUJI MEDIUMS.
OO (LOOM)

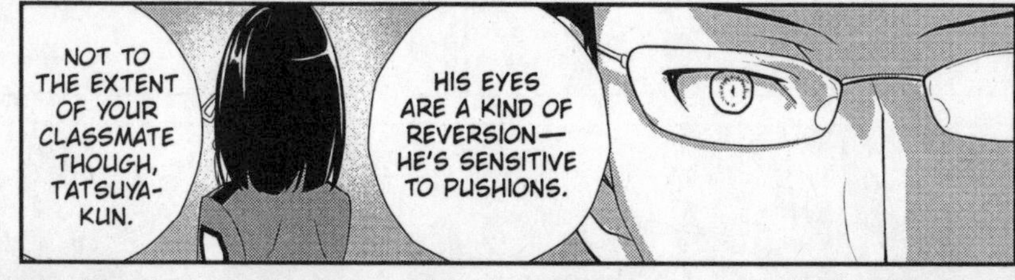
HIS EYES ARE A KIND OF REVERSION— HE'S SENSITIVE TO PUSHIONS.
NOT TO THE EXTENT OF YOUR CLASSMATE THOUGH, TATSUYA-KUN.

IN FACT, MORE IMPORTANT IS HIS OLDER STEPBROTHER, HAJIME, WHOM HIS MOTHER'S SECOND HUSBAND BROUGHT WITH HIM WHEN THEY MARRIED.
KINOE WAS MADE TO ENROLL AT FIRST HIGH AS HIS PUPPET.

AND THIS HAJIME TSUKASA...
...IS THE LEADER OF THE JAPANESE BRANCH OF BLANCHE...
...AND MANAGES ALL OPERATIONS, COVERT AND OTHERWISE.
!!
TO BE CONTINUED IN VOLUME 4

HARD TO
SEE FACE
SUNDAY
BEST
COMPLETELY
FORTIFIED!!
LONG
LENGTH

**◉ Activation sequence**
The blueprints for magic and the programs used to construct it. Activation sequence data is stored in a compressed format in C.A.D.s. Design waves are sent from the magician to the device, where they are converted into a signal according to the decompressed data and returned to the magician.

**◉ Antinite**
A military-grade commodity produced only in lands where ancient alpine civilizations prospered, such as parts of the Aztec empire and the Mayan countries and regions. Extremely valuable due to its limited production quantity and impossible for civilians to acquire.

**◉ Blooms, Weeds**
Terms displaying the gap between Course 1 students and Course 2 students in First High. The left breast of Course 1 student uniforms is emblazoned with an eight-petaled emblem, but it is absent from the Course 2 uniforms.

**◉ Cabinets**
Small, linear vehicles holding either two or four passengers and controlled by a central station. Used for commuting to work and school as a public transportation replacement for trains.

**◉ C.A.D. (Casting Assistant Device)**
A device that simplifies the activation of magic. Magical programming is recorded inside. The main types are specialized and all-purpose.

**◉ Cast jamming**
A variety of typeless magic that obstructs magic programs from exerting influence on Eidos. It weakens the process by which magic programs affect Eidos by scattering large amounts of meaningless psionic waves.

**◉ Eidos (individual information bodies)**
Originally a term from Greek philosophy. In modern magic, "Eidos" are the bodies of information that accompany phenomena. They record the existence of those phenomena on the world, so they can also be called the footprints that phenomena leave on the world. The term "magic" in modern magic refers to the technology that modifies these phenomena by modifying Eidos.

**◉ Four Leaves Technology (F.L.T.)**
A domestic C.A.D. manufacturer. Originally famous for its magic engineering equipment rather than finished C.A.D.s, but with the development of its Silver line of models, its fame skyrocketed as a C.A.D. manufacturer.

**◉ Idea (information body dimension)**
Pronounced "ee-dee-ah." Originally a term from Greek philosophy. In modern magic, "Idea" refers to the platform on which Eidos are recorded. Magic's primary form is a technology wherein a magic program is output onto this platform, thus rewriting the Eidos recorded within.

**◉ Loopcast system**
An activation sequence made so that a magician can continually execute a spell as many times as their calculation capacity will permit. Normally, one must re-expand activation sequences from the C.A.D. every time one executes the same spell, but the loopcast system makes it possible to avoid this time-consuming repetition by automatically duplicating the activation program's final state in the magician's magic calculation region.

**◉ Magic Association of Japan**
A social group of Japanese magicians, with its headquarters in Kyoto. The Kantou branch location is established within Yokohama Bay Hills Tower.

◉ **Magic calculation region**
A mental region for the construction of magic sequences. The substance, so to speak, of magical talent. It exists in a magician's unconscious, and even if a magician is normally aware of using his or her magic calculation region, he or she cannot be aware of the processes being conducted within. The magic calculation region can be called a "black box" for the magician himself.

◉ **Magic engineer**
Refers to engineers who design, develop, and maintain an apparatus that assists, amplifies, and strengthens magic. Their reputation in society is slightly worse than that of magicians. However, magic engineers are indispensable for tuning the C.A.D.s, indispensable tools for magicians, so in the industrial world, they're in higher demand than normal magicians. A first-rate magic engineer's earnings surpass that of even first-rate magicians.

◉ **Magic High School**
The nickname for the high schools affiliated with the National Magic University. There are nine established throughout the country. Of them, the first through the third have two hundred students per grade and use the Course 1/Course 2 system.

◉ **Magic sequence**
An information body for the purpose of temporarily altering information attached to phenomena. They are constructed from the Psions possessed by magicians.

◉ **Magician**
An abbreviation of "magical technician." A magical technician is the name for anyone with the skill to use magic at a practical level.

◉ **Nine School Competition**
An abbreviation of "National Magic High School Goodwill Magic Competition Tournament." Magic high school students throughout the country, from First through Ninth High, are gathered to compete with their schools in fierce magic showdowns. There are six events: Speed Shooting, Cloudball, Battle Board, Ice Pillars Break, Mirage Bat, and Monolith Code.

◉ **Psions**
Non-physical particles belonging to the dimension of psychic phenomena. Psions are elements that record information on consciousness and thought products.
Eidos (the theoretical basis for modern magic) as well as activation sequences and magic sequences—supporting its main framework—are all bodies of information constructed from Psions.

◉ **Pushions**
Non-physical particles belonging to the dimension of psychic phenomena. Their existence has been proven, but their true form and functions have yet to be elucidated. Magicians are generally able to only "feel" the pushions being activated through magic.

THE
HONOR
STUDENT
AT
Magic High
School

HEY THERE! GIRL DETECTIVES HERE!
I didn't expect things to be that dangerous ...
THE TRAUMA...
IT WAS INDEED AN EVENT THAT TURNS A LIGHT NOVEL INTO A HEAVY ONE!
STOP! WE CAN'T SAY ANY MORE!
ANYWAY, THERE'S A MYSTERY I WANT TO SOLVE, AND—
AMY'S HAIR I—
GA (CLAMP)
WE CAN'T SAY ANY MORE!
THEY DECIDED ON THE CHARACTER DESIGNS FOR THE ANIME.
Special Thanks
SATO-SENSEI ISHIDA-SAMA JIMMY STONE-SAMA ISHIMOTO-SAMA
KITAUMI-SENSEI HAYASHI-SENSEI TANAKA-SAMA, THE EDITOR TOMIYAMA-SAMA
ENDOU-SAMA KANEKO-SAMA MAEDA-SAMA
PLEASE CONTINUE TO SUPPORT ME!
YU MORI

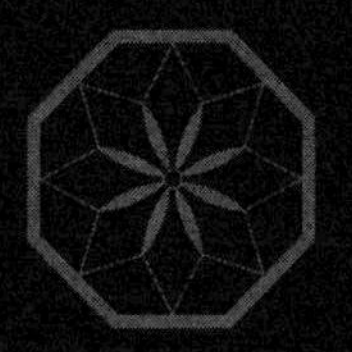

THE HONOR STUDENT
AT MAGIC HIGH SCHOOL

SPECIAL CONTRIBUTION

Mori-sensei, congratulations on the release of the third volume of *The Honor Student at Magic High School.*

To me, the episodes recorded herein strongly complement the original work, boldly cutting scenes that were once there and fitting new pieces into the story that bring new colors to the fore. It's quite difficult to make everything match for complementary narratives like this, but I felt that this volume accomplished the task with charming—even sexy—aplomb.

Miyuki, as drawn by Mori-sensei, is a classic "beauty" character with just as much charm as the other girls, but I'm so happy her chilly side got a chance to appear. She tends to hide behind her attachment to her brother, but she's no cupcake. Quite the contrary, she has an almost shockingly cruel aspect to her personality. Not because she's secretly traumatized or anything—it's simply the worldview she was raised with, the result of her upbringing, and this chilliness, too, is an important part of the character. The fact that it was so thoroughly depicted at every turn filled me with a satisfaction I thought I could get only when I was the one writing. The difference between Honoka's and Shizuku's reactions after hearing Miyuki's "confession" were also funny. The other characters would have acted like this:

Erika: ...It really doesn't sound like you're joking.
Leo: ...Ooh, scary.
Mizuki: Er, umm...Is that so?
Mikihiko: ... (I wonder if I can pretend I didn't hear that.)

...Or something like that, at least.

—Oh, Tatsuya?

"Tatsuya...I am a coldhearted woman."

"I know that, Miyuki. I also know that, more than that, you're a kind little sister," he'd probably say, without even batting an eye.

...No, that won't work. Out of context it just makes him sound like a gigolo (nervous sweat).

I'll think I'll leave the unamusing skits at that.

Mori-sensei, I look forward to the next volume.

佐島勤
Tsutomu Sato

**Congratulations on the release of *Honor Student* Volume 3!**

I'm so sorry for changing her hairstyle!

**Amy-chan in the manga is so lively and cute, so I drew her. Wonderful!**

CONGRATULATIONS
ON THE RELEASE OF
HONOR STUDENT VOLUME 3!
きたうみつな
TSUNA KITAUMI
THIS IS HAYASHI, THE ONE WHO DOES THE ADAPTATION FOR THE GF MANGA VERSION OF
THE IRREGULAR AT MAGIC HIGH SCHOOL.
CONGRATULATIONS ON THE RELEASE OF THE THIRD VOLUME OF HONOR STUDENT!
AMID THE UNSETTLING AIR IN THE TENSE SCHOOL, MIYUKI'S EXPRESSIONS OF DISTRESS AS SHE THOUGHT OF HER BROTHER WERE SO CHARMING!
ESPECIALLY WHEN SHE LEARNED THAT HONOKA AND THE OTHERS WERE TAKING SECRET PICTURES OF TATSUYA.
THE SCENE WHERE SHE MUMBLES "I'M JEALOUS!" MADE MY HEART SKIP A BEAT (LOL), SO CUTE...!
MIYUKI'S NOT THE ONLY ONE THOUGH—AMY, HONOKA, AND SHIZUKU, THE GIRL DETECTIVES, ARE SO CUTE I CAN'T STAND IT.
I'LL CONTINUE TO ENJOY ALL OF THEIR CHARMING VITALITY FLOWING FROM EVERY VOLUME AND TRY MY BEST TO GET PUMPED UP RIGHT ALONG WITH THEM!
FUMINO HAYASHI

THE HONOR STUDENT AT Magic High School

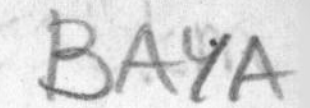

# THE HONOR STUDENT AT MAGIC HIGH SCHOOL ❸

**YU MORI**
**Original Story: TSUTOMU SATO**
**Character Design: KANA ISHIDA**

**Translation: Andrew Prowse**
**Lettering: Phil Christie**




Edited by ASCII MEDIA WORKS
First published in Japan in 2014 by KADOKAWA CORPORATION, Tokyo.
English translation rights arranged with KADOKAWA CORPORATION, Tokyo, through Tuttle-Mori Agency, Inc., Tokyo.



Yen Press
Hachette Book Group
1290 Avenue of the Americas
New York, NY 10104

www.hachettebookgroup.com
www.yenpress.com

Yen Press is an imprint of Hachette Book Group, Inc.
The Yen Press name and logo are trademarks of Hachette Book Group, Inc.

The publisher is not responsible for websites (or their content) not owned by the publisher.

Library of Congress Control Number: 2016932699

First Yen Press Edition: June 2016

ISBN: 978-0-316-39035-4

10 9 8 7 6 5 4 3 2 1

BVG

Printed in the United States of America